CAT
Got Your
Tongue?

CAT Got Your Tongue?

CURIOUS FELINE PHRASES
from Around the World

Hannah Shaw

Illustrations by
SOPHIE LUCIDO JOHNSON

Ten Speed Press
California | New York

For my
sweet, chatty cat,
Haroun.

INTRODUCTION

*T*he English language is filled with feline phrases. When we reveal a secret, we *let the cat out of the bag.* When we caution our friends not to be too inquisitive, we remind them that *curiosity killed the cat.* And when we really like something, we might even say it's *the cat's pajamas*! These proverbs and idioms are so commonplace that sometimes we forget about the absurdity of what is being said. Since when do cats wear pajamas, anyway?

Cats truly have a way of grabbing our attention. After rescuing a little kitten I'd found in a treetop many years ago, my priorities completely shifted . . . and I dedicated my life to saving cats and changing the way we perceive and treat the most vulnerable felines. I've come to believe that the way we speak about animals has a large impact on the way we understand who they are and what they need. For this reason, I've long been interested in the presence of these magnificent creatures in figurative language—but it wasn't until I began to work internationally with cats that I gained insight into their ubiquity in expressions around the globe.

As my husband and I traveled to Nepal, Italy, Japan, Kenya, Chile, and dozens of other countries to do research and take photographs for our book *Cats of the World,* I made it a habit to ask local advocates about cat-related sayings in their native languages. To my delight, I was introduced to an absolute treasure trove of cat-centered proverbs and idioms that ranged from beautifully insightful to downright hilarious! It was fascinating to find that, despite linguistic differences, we share so many common principles, often expressed through a feline frame of reference.

Perhaps it should come as no surprise that cats have captured our collective imagination and caught our global tongue. Cats have been integrated into human societies since the dawn of civilization, when *Felis catus* became a symbiotic partner for early settlers, who valued them for their prowess in protecting crops from rodents. As seafarers and merchants explored the world, cats went along for the ride . . . and began to spread both their populations and their influence across the map. Cats are as much a part of the human story as storytelling itself.

With transcontinental exploration came the dissemination not only of living beings such as cats and humans but also of fables, folklore, and oral traditions. Ancient stories, like *Aesop's Fables,* traveled throughout the world, being reinterpreted time and time again to reflect the local cultural customs, social mores, and linguistic styles. Like a game of telephone, many of these stories inspired short phrases that could quickly represent a complex moral teaching or concept . . . and it's fascinating to realize just how many of these sayings involve cats!

Take, for instance, the medieval fable "Belling the Cat," in which a group of mice agrees that the best way to ensure their collective safety is to place a bell around the neck of the cat. Their plan sounds perfect, but there is just one problem: Which mouse is brave enough for the task? This fable, told and retold, now takes the form of shortened idioms in many cultures; the Hindi idiom *billi ke gale mein ghanti bandhna* (bell the cat) represents a group agreeing to perform an impossibly difficult task, while the French *attacher le grelot* (to attach the bell [to the cat]) is used to describe the act of taking one for the team. That an ancient fable finds its remnants in such diverse languages is a testament to the power of the proverbial, uniting us all through shared wisdom about the human condition that has been passed down through generations and across cultures.

Over and over, cats find their place in our figurative expressions, often as a proxy for the human subject, or sometimes as the subject's foil. In many proverbs, it's the cat's relationship to his or her prey that makes the metaphor work; the temptation of the hunt, and the cat's cunning prowess or utter failure, serve as suitable stand-ins for our own experiences of desire, success, and defeat. It's clear that we can see ourselves in the eyes of a cat . . . and sometimes we may even imagine ourselves as the prey.

The representation of cats in the phrases I've collected is undeniably variable. In some cases, they embody positive attributes such as agility and independence, while in others they take on unfavorable traits such as corruptibility and deceit. In many ways their character is paradoxical: they are written as clever or foolish, brave or fearful, clean or messy, and of high or low status. And while I personally have only the warmest feelings toward our feline friends, I must admit that it's the complex nature of cats that makes them so easy to identify with, and to adore!

The old English proverb, *A cat may look at a king,* serves as a poignant reminder that, regardless of their status in the world, every individual holds fundamental rights and intrinsic value—that even the tiniest cat is inherently worthy. How magical that this centuries-old teaching, first published in *The Proverbs of John Heywood* (1546), then again in Lewis Carroll's *Alice's Adventures in Wonderland* (1865), now finds a modern home here in my collection of feline-focused phrases from around the world. It is truly a marvel that a creature so small has such great power to not only enrich our lives with comforting purrs and playful antics, but to also sprinkle our languages with such profound, timeless wisdom.

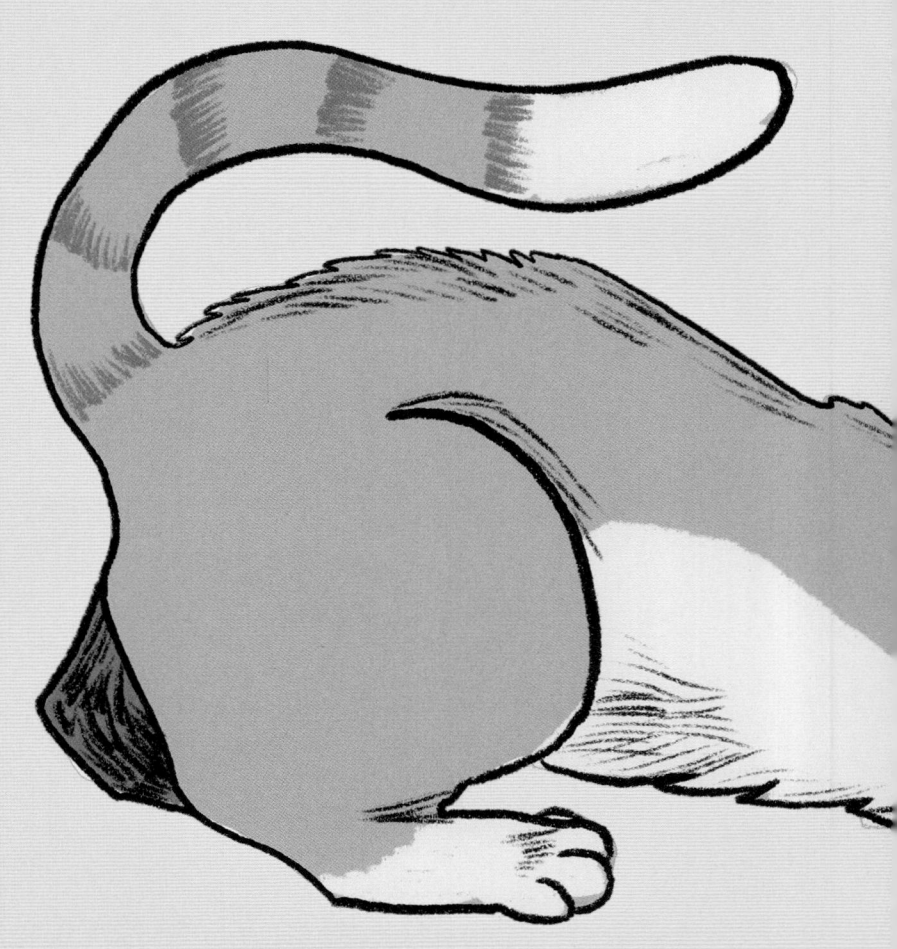

the FIRST CATS
over the fence

Polish

Pierwsze koty za płoty

USE: To describe a first attempt at doing something difficult, as it will rarely be perfect, but subsequent attempts will be better; similar to "the first pancake is always spoiled."

Farsi

این عبارت یک ضرب المثل فارسی اس.

**Gorbe dastesh be goosht nemirese,
mige boo mideh.**

USE: To describe one who is suppressing their
desire for something inaccessible to them by
claiming they didn't want it anyway; similar
to "sour grapes."

A kitten can only catch a BABY MOUSE.

Ewe

Ðadi vi afi vi wòlena.

MEANING: Don't overestimate yourself;
be realistic about what you can achieve.

May you turn into a BLINTZ and be snatched by a cat.

Yiddish

וערן זאָל פֿון דיר אַ בלינטשיק און
די קאַץ זאָל דיך כאַפֿן◊

**Vern zol fun dir a blintshik,
un di kats zol dikh khapn.**

USE: A spiteful expression wishing harm.

Japanese

猫舌

Nekojita

USE: A term for a person who can't handle hot food or drinks; for instance, "You've already finished your ramen, and I'm still waiting for mine to cool down; I'm a nekojita!"

Irish Gaelic

Go n-ithe an cat thú is go n-ithe an Diabhal an cat.

USE: A curse expressing ill will.

May the cat eat you, and may THE DEVIL eat the cat.

[TO GO] under a CAT'S TAIL

Russian

Коту под хвост

Kotu pod khvost

USE: To describe something that has been done in vain or gone to waste; similar to "down the drain" or "out the window."

TO BUY a cat in a sack

German

Die Katze im Sack kaufen

MEANING: To make a risky purchase without inspecting it first; similar to buying "a pig in a poke."

Welsh

Fel cath i gythraul

MEANING: At top speed; similar to "like a bat out of hell."

Swedish

Gå som katten kring het gröt

MEANING: To avoid addressing an issue directly; similar to "beat around the bush."

To walk like the cat around HOT porridge

Cat's COUGH

Croatian

Mačji kašalj

USE: To describe a very easy task;
similar to "a piece of cake."

Like a CAT CRIED

Ukrainian

Як кіт наплакав

Yak kit naplakav

USE: To describe something very low in quantity; similar to "a drop in the ocean."

German

**Nur einen Katzensprung
entfernt sein**

MEANING: To be very close by;
similar to "a stone's throw."

A CAT'S house

Russian

Кошкин дом

Koshkin dom

MEANING: A very messy
place; similar to "a pigsty."

French

Donner sa langue au chat

MEANING: To give up your attempt at a guess because you don't know the answer; one might respond to a riddle with "I have no idea, I give my tongue to the cat."

The trap set for THE RABBIT caught the cat.

Burmese

ယုန်ထောင် ကြောင်မိ.

Yonehtaung kyaung mi.

MEANING: The actions taken didn't have the intended result.

The handwriting looks like a cat's SCRATCH.

Vietnamese

Chữ viết như mèo quào.

MEANING: The handwriting looks almost illegible; similar to "like chicken scratch."

Hindi

ऊँट के गले में बिल्ली

Uṅṭ ke gale meṅ billī

MEANING: An unreasonable precondition, as in a sneaky clause in fine print; derives from a folk tale about a man who says he will sell his camel for a penny, but then ties a cat to the camel's neck and charges much more for the cat.

English (Scottish dialect)

Has yer cat deid?

USE: To insult the length of someone's pants, as if to say, "Your pants are so short, it looks like you're flying a flag at half-mast."

You have the cat by the TAIL.

Afrikaans

Jy het die kat aan die stert beet.

MEANING: You have absolutely no idea what you're doing.

The HASTY CAT gave birth to blind kittens.

Italian

La gatta frettolosa ha fatto i figli ciechi.

MEANING: If you rush, you might not have the desired outcome; similar to "haste makes waste."

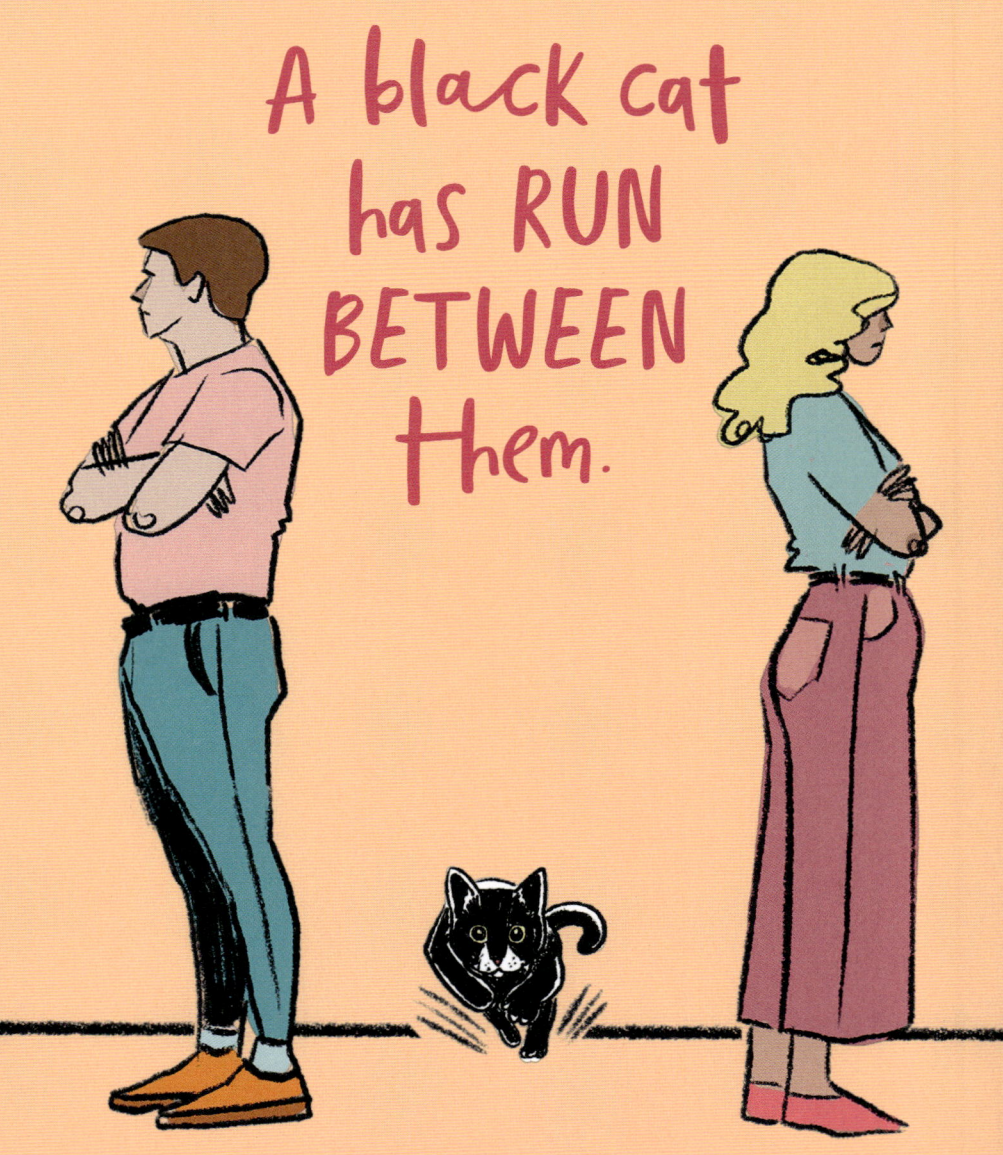

Yiddish

עס איז דורכגעלאָפֿן צווישן זיי אַ
שווּאַרצע קאַץ◊

**Es iz durkhgelofn tsvishn zey a
shvartse kats.**

MEANING: The relationship has soured.

Russian

Уйти от кота и попасть под метлу

Uyti ot kota i popast' pod metlu

MEANING: To go from bad to worse; similar to "out of the frying pan, into the fire."

Afrikaans

Katjie van die baan

USE: To describe someone who is social and fun; similar to "life of the party."

To tie the cat to the BACON

Dutch

De kat op het spek binden

MEANING: To forbid something that is extremely tempting; for example, to leave children unsupervised with a cookie jar they're not permitted to open.

Kitten

Czech

Kočičko

USE: A pet name for someone you love, similar to "sweetheart."

Finnish

Konstit on monet, sano mummo, kun kissalla pöytää pyyhki.

MEANING: There's more than one way to get the job done; similar to "there's more than one way to skin a cat."

There are many ways, said grandma, while WIPING the table with a cat.

[IT'S LIKE] Asking a CAT to take care of

THE FISH

Korean

고양이에게 생선을 맡기다

Goyangiege saengseoneul matgida

MEANING: Entrusting someone with a task that is counter to their personal interests, knowing that they likely won't do it properly; similar to "a fox guarding the hen house."

Nepali

दुधको साक्षी बिरालो.

Dudhko sākṣī birālo.

MEANING: The testimony is unreliable because the witness can't be trusted, just as you couldn't trust a cat to tell you the truth about what happened to the milk.

Czech

V noci každá kočka černá.

USE: To describe a literal low-light setting where distinctions aren't apparent and appearances have lost their significance, or a situation where one is figuratively in the dark and struggles to make an assessment due to a lack of clarity.

TO LOOK the cat out of the tree

Dutch

De kat uit de boom kijken

MEANING: To wait and see how a situation develops before taking any action; similar to "see which way the wind blows."

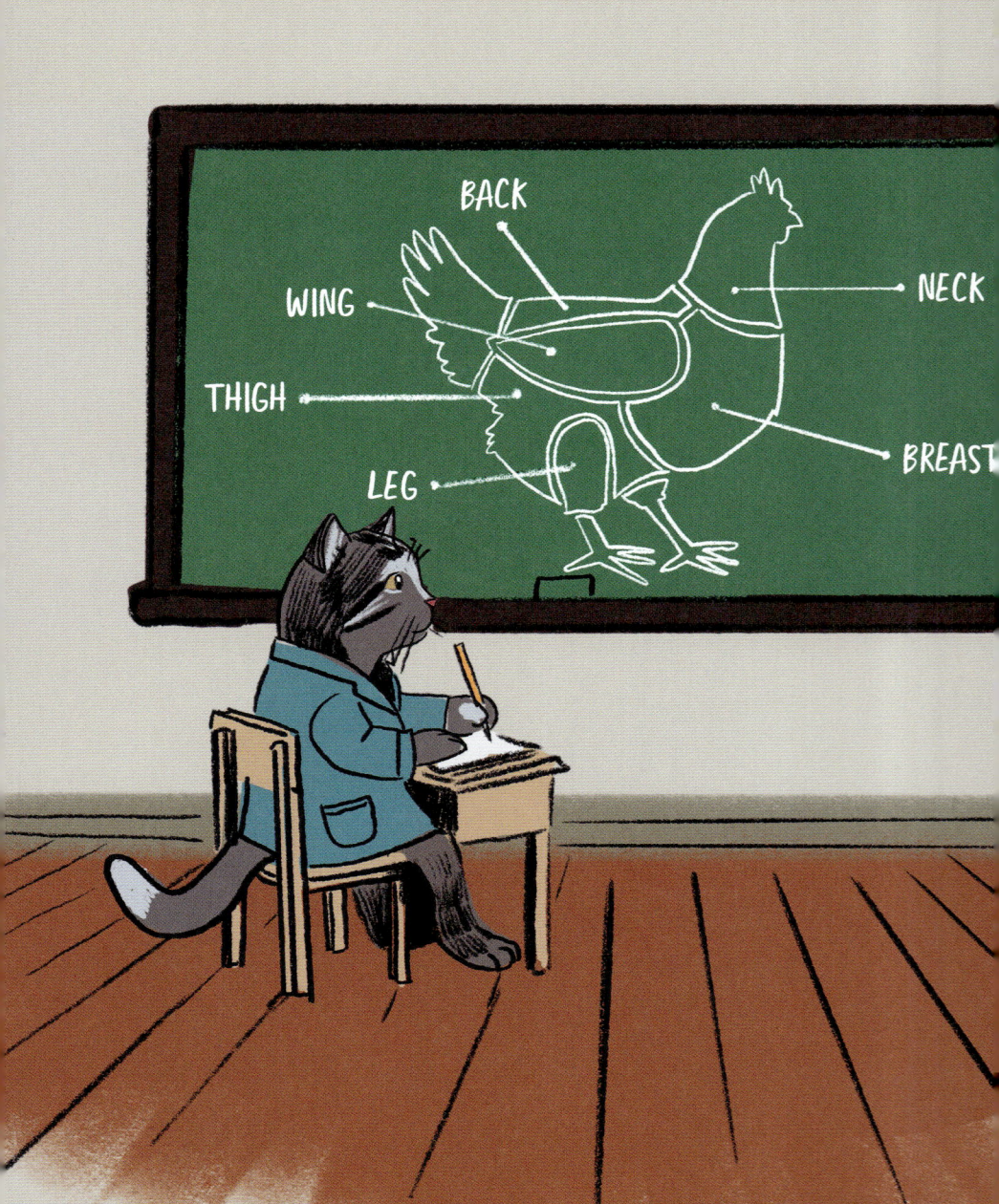

If we learned by LOOKING, cats would be butchers.

Turkish

Bakarak öğrenilseydi, kediler kasap olurdu.

MEANING: You can't learn everything just by observing.

Indonesian

Malu-malu kucing

USE: To describe someone who acts too shy to do something—despite actually wanting to—often to be polite and modest when receiving an offer.

Traditional Chinese

三腳貓功夫

Sān jiǎo māo gōngfū

USE: To mock the incompetence of a person who has inadequate skills; for instance, to poke fun at someone who made a failed attempt at a DIY project.

Cat with HORSESHOES

Greek

Γάτα με πέταλα

Gata me petala

MEANING: A sharp, clever, quick-witted person.

The cat who lives to EAT

Traditional Chinese

為食貓

Wèi shí māo

USE: To describe a greedy, gluttonous person.

Portuguese

Gato escaldado tem medo de água fria.

MEANING: One who has had a bad experience tends to become cautious, even in situations that may not be harmful; similar to "once bitten, twice shy."

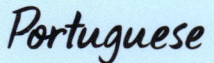

Croatian

Doće maca na vratanca.

USE: A warning that a person will someday face the consequences of their actions; similar to "what goes around comes around," with the connotation that a small misdeed can have large repercussions.

To send
one's CAT

Flemish

Zijn kat sturen

MEANING: To not show up for an appointment, as in: "I was supposed to meet with my colleague today, but he sent his cat."

The cat WEEPS for the dead mouse.

Traditional Chinese

貓哭老鼠.

Māo kū lǎo shǔ.

USE: To describe the act of pretending to be sympathetic or compassionate; similar to "crocodile tears."

To act like a DEAD CAT

Italian

Fare la gatta morta

USE: A pejorative used to describe a woman who acts innocent or naive but is actually being manipulative or seductive.

Russian

Не всё коту масленица.

Ne vsyo kotu Maslenitsa.

MEANING: Not every moment is filled with joy and happiness; similar to "it's not all sunshine and rainbows," but specifically referring to Maslenitsa, an Eastern Slavic holiday during which pancakes are eaten.

We MENTIONED
the cat, and he
came and jumped.

Arabic

جبنا سيرة القط جه ينط.

.gebna seerat el qitt gah Yenott

MEANING: Merely talking about a subject has lead to its occurrence or appearance; similar to "speak of the devil."

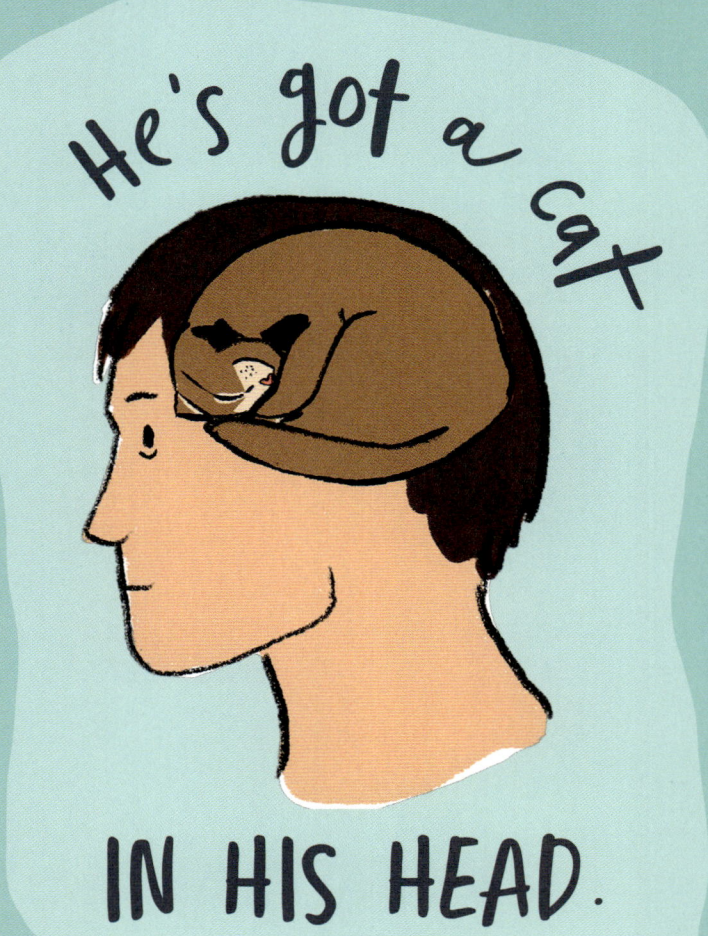

Yiddish

ער האָט אַ קאַצנקאָפֿ◊

Er hot a katsnkop.

MEANING: He can't remember anything.

A mouse does not RUN INTO a sleeping cat's MOUTH.

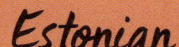

Estonian

Magavale kassile hiir suhu ei jookse.

MEANING: Laziness won't get you where you want to be; similar to "no pain, no gain."

Japanese

猫の手も借りたい.

Neko no te mo karitai.

MEANING: I'm so overwhelmed,
I need all the help I can get.

Oh, DARN CAT!

Norwegian

Å, fyttikatta!

USE: To convey surprise or mild frustration; a strong but innocent expletive similar to "oh my goodness!"

To look [AT SOMETHING] like the cat at A CALENDAR

Romanian

A se uita ca mâța-n calendar

MEANING: To appear very confused.

Don't look for FIVE FEET on the cat.

Spanish

No le busques cinco pies al gato.

MEANING: Don't overcomplicate things or look for a problem that isn't there; similar to "don't make a mountain out of a molehill."

To place someone before THE NOSE OF A CAT

Icelandic

**Að koma einhverjum
fyrir kattarnef**

MEANING: To murder someone.

Hungarian

A macska rúgja meg!

MEANING: Damn it!

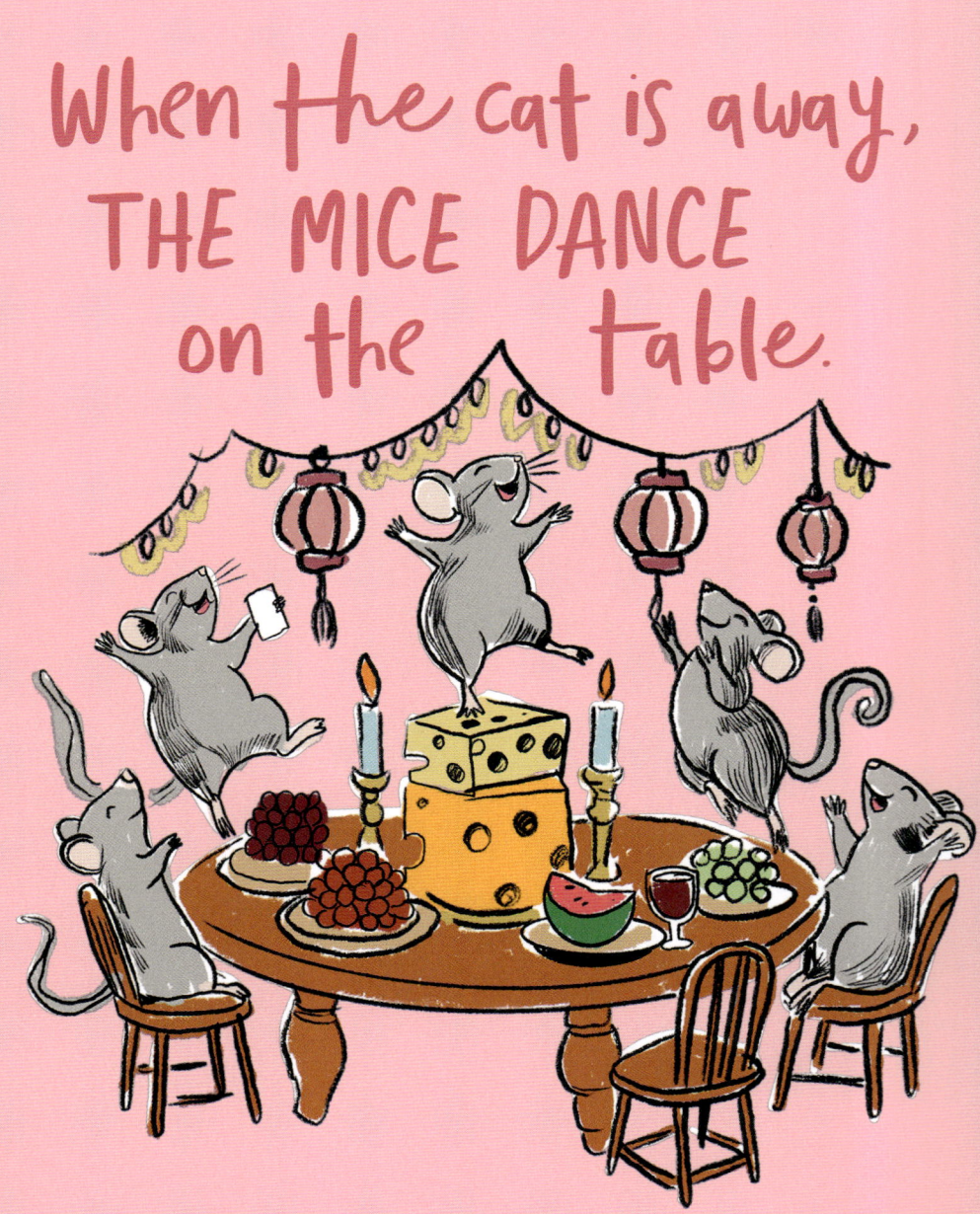

German

Wenn die Katze aus dem Haus ist, tanzen die Mäuse auf dem Tisch.

MEANING: When the authority figure isn't looking, people will misbehave; similar to "when the cat's away, the mice will play."

Who lifts the cat's tail if not the CAT ITSELF?

Finnish

Kuka kissan hännän nostaa ellei kissa itse?

MEANING: You should speak highly of your own accomplishments; similar to "toot your own horn."

Cat's
FOREHEAD

Japanese

猫の額

Neko no hitai

USE: To describe a very narrow space, such as a small apartment or garden, as in: "I would offer to host a party, but there's not enough room; my new condo is a cat's forehead."

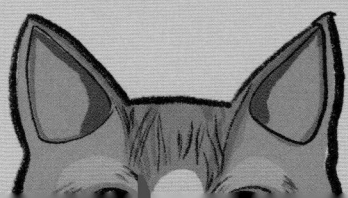

Like a cat with SEVEN SOULS

Arabic

متل القط بسبع رواح

ruah bisabe alqati Mutalu

USE: To describe someone who has been through a lot of challenges but has managed to cope well.

Simplified Chinese

猫改不了偷腥.

Māo gǎi bù liǎo tōu xīng.

USE: To describe a person whose habits are deeply engrained and unlikely to change. Often used to describe or justify the behavior of men, similar to "boys will be boys."

Malay

Kucing lalu, tikus tiada berdecit lagi.

MEANING: In the presence of an authority figure or threat, a loud person becomes quiet.

It's CAT PEE.

French

C'est du pipi de chat.

MEANING: It's not very important;
similar to "small potatoes."

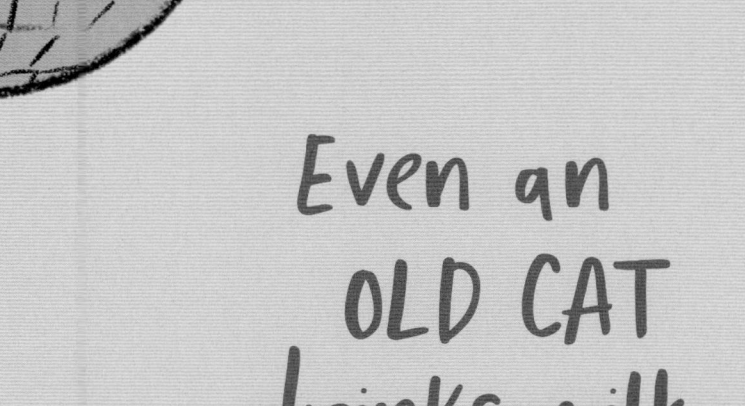

Even an OLD CAT drinks milk.

Swahili

Hata paka mzee hunywa maziwa.

MEANING: Some habits never change, regardless of age; often used to describe seniors who like to dance or party.

Spanish

Hay cuatro gatos.

MEANING: There is very low
attendance at this event.

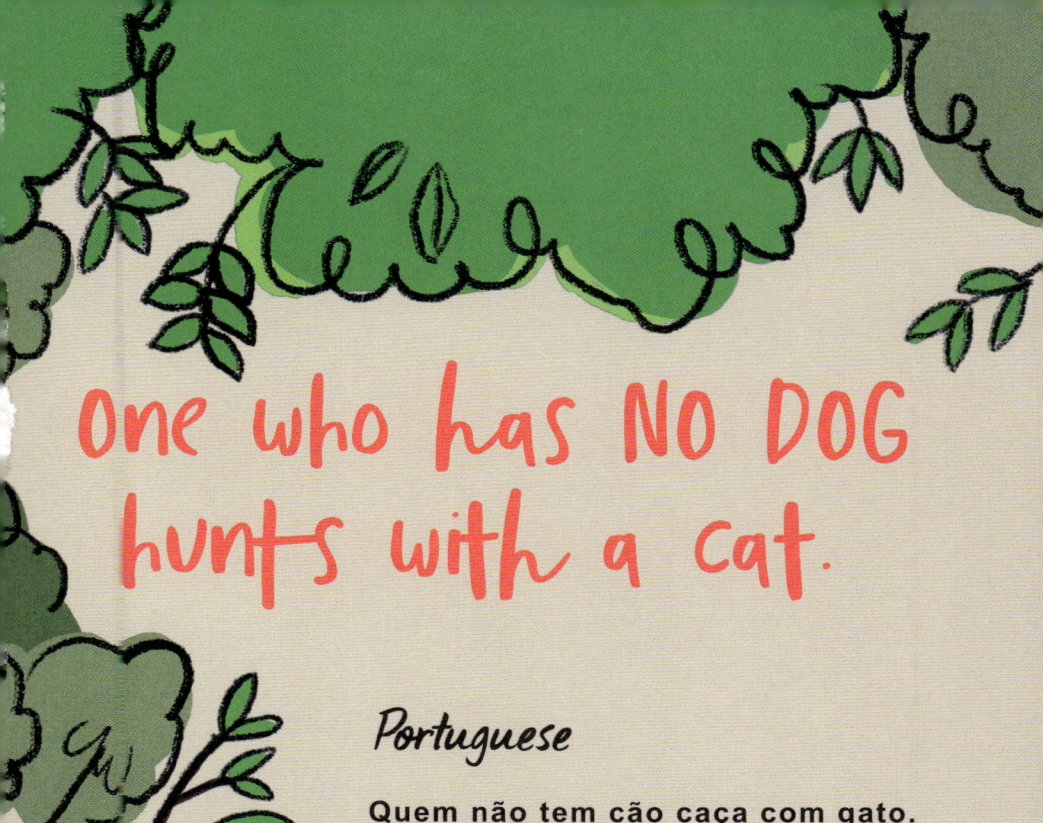

One who has NO DOG hunts with a cat.

Portuguese

Quem não tem cão caça com gato.

MEANING: We must make do with the resources we have, even if they aren't ideal.

I care like a cat cares that it's WEDNESDAY.

Yiddish

עס אַרט מיך ווי דער
פֿאַראַיאָריקער שניי◇

**Es art mikh vi der
farayoriker shney.**

MEANING: I don't care at all.

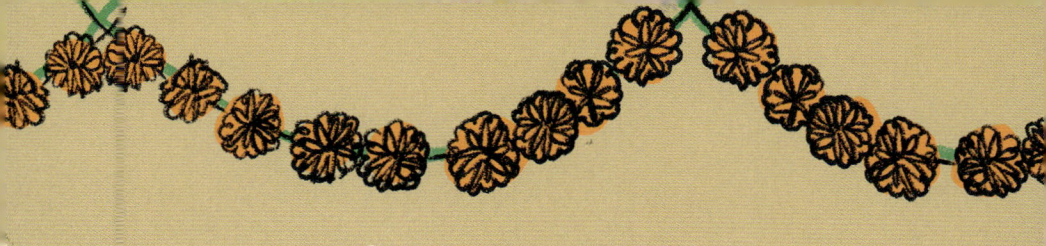

After eating NINE HUNDRED mice, the cat goes on a pilgrimage.

Hindi

नौ सौ चूहे खाकर बिल्ली हज को चली।

Nau sau chuḥe khākar billī haj ko chalī.

USE: To describe someone who creates a facade of goodness to compensate for their immoral deeds.

Spanish

Aquí hay gato encerrado.

MEANING: Something is hidden or isn't being said; similar to "there's something fishy about this."

As nervous as a
LONG-TAILED CAT
in a room full of
rocking chairs

English

MEANING: Extremely (and perhaps rightfully) nervous.

THE CAT and the RAT
sleep together.

Simplified Chinese

猫鼠同眠.

Māo shǔ tóng mián.

USE: To describe acts of collusion, such as corrupt officials shielding one another.

ABOUT THE AUTHOR

Hannah Shaw, also known as Kitten lady, is an award-winning kitten rescuer, humane educator, and unwavering animal advocate who has dedicated her life to innovating kitten care and protecting the most vulnerable felines. She is the *New York Times* bestselling author of *Tiny but Mighty, Cats of the World, Kitten Lady's Big Book of Little Kittens, Kitten Lady's CATivity Book,* and the Adventures in Fosterland series. She is also the founder of Orphan Kitten Club, a national 501(c)(3) nonprofit organization saving the lives of neonatal kittens. She lives in California with her husband, their cats and dog, and an endless rotation of foster animals.

Published in the United States by Ten Speed Press, an imprint of the Crown Publishing
Group, a division of Penguin Random House LLC, New York.
TenSpeed.com

Typefaces: Set Sail Studio's Totally Terrific, Hanoded's Uncle Edward and Pandanus,
Linotype's Trade Gothic, and Monotype's Arial Unicode.

Library of Congress Cataloging-in-Publication Data
Names: Shaw, Hannah René, 1987- author. I Johnson, Sophie Lucido, illustrator.
Title: Cat got your tongue? : curious feline phrases from around the world / Hannah
Shaw ; illustrations by Sophie Lucido Johnson. Identifiers: LCCN 2024025592
(print) I LCCN 2024025593 (ebook) I ISBN 9780593836385 (hardcover) I ISBN
9780593836392 (ebook) Subjects: LCSH: Cats—Pictorial works. I Cats—Miscellanea.
I Idioms. Classification: LCC SF446 .S48 2025 (print) I LCC SF446 (ebook) I DDC
398.9—dc23/eng/20241128
LC record available at https://lccn.loc.gov/2024025592
LC ebook record available at https://lccn.loc.gov/2024025593

Hardcover ISBN: 978-0-593-83638-5
Ebook ISBN: 978-0-593-83639-2

Printed in China

Editor: Julie Bennett
Production editors: Ashley Pierce and Taylor Teague
Designer: Francesca Truman I Art director: Betsy Stromberg
Production designer: Mari Gill I Production manager: Jane Chinn
Copyeditor: Amelia Ayrelan Iuvino I Proofreader: Surina Jain
Publicist: Natalie Yera-Campbell I Marketer: Andrea Portanova

10 9 8 7 6 5 4 3 2 1

First Edition